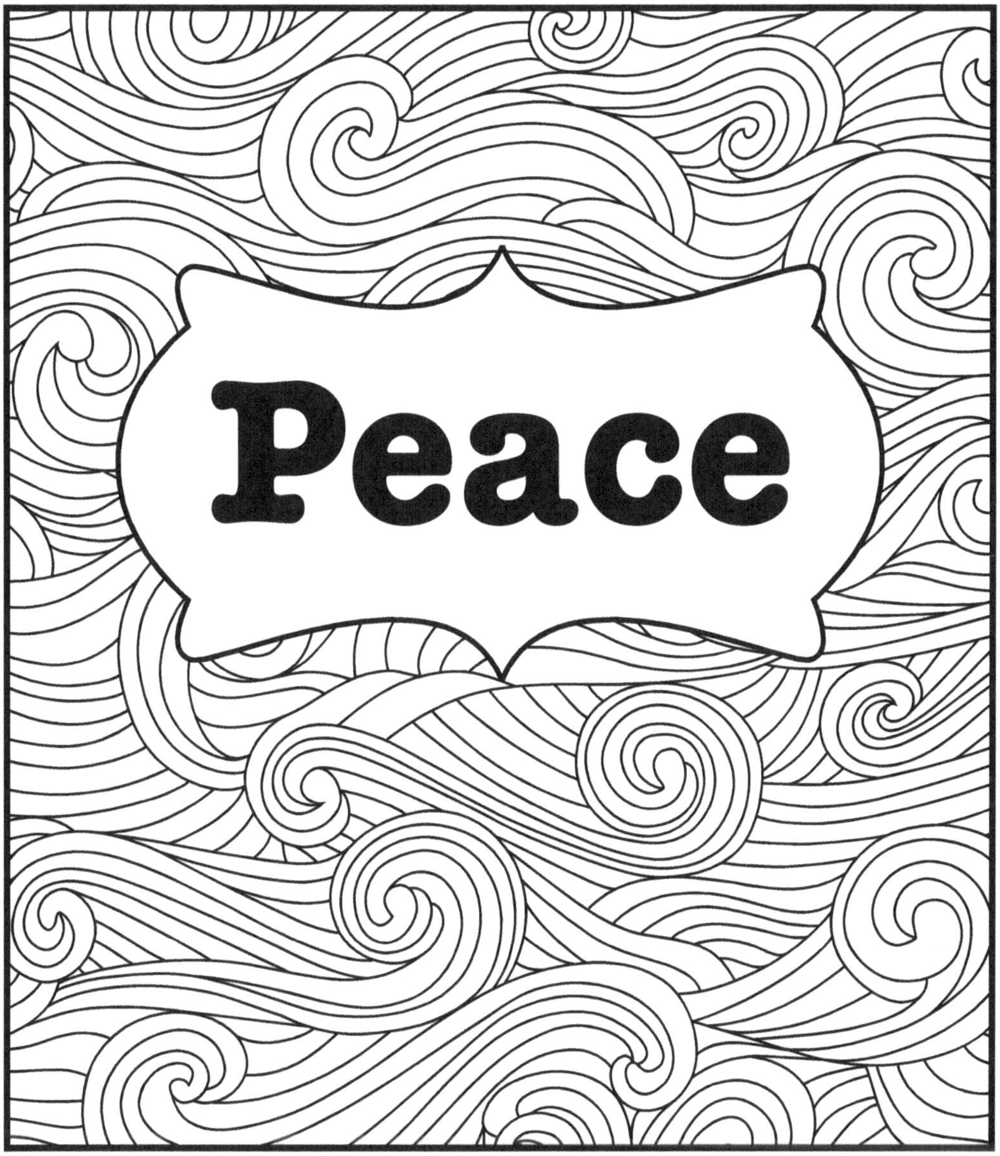

Completely **Calming** Colouring Book 1

First published in 2015 by Kyle Craig Publishing

Editor: Alison McNicol

Cover Design: Julie Anson

ISBN: 978-1-78595-072-8

A CIP record for this book is available from the British Library.

A Kyle Craig Publication

www.kyle-craig.com

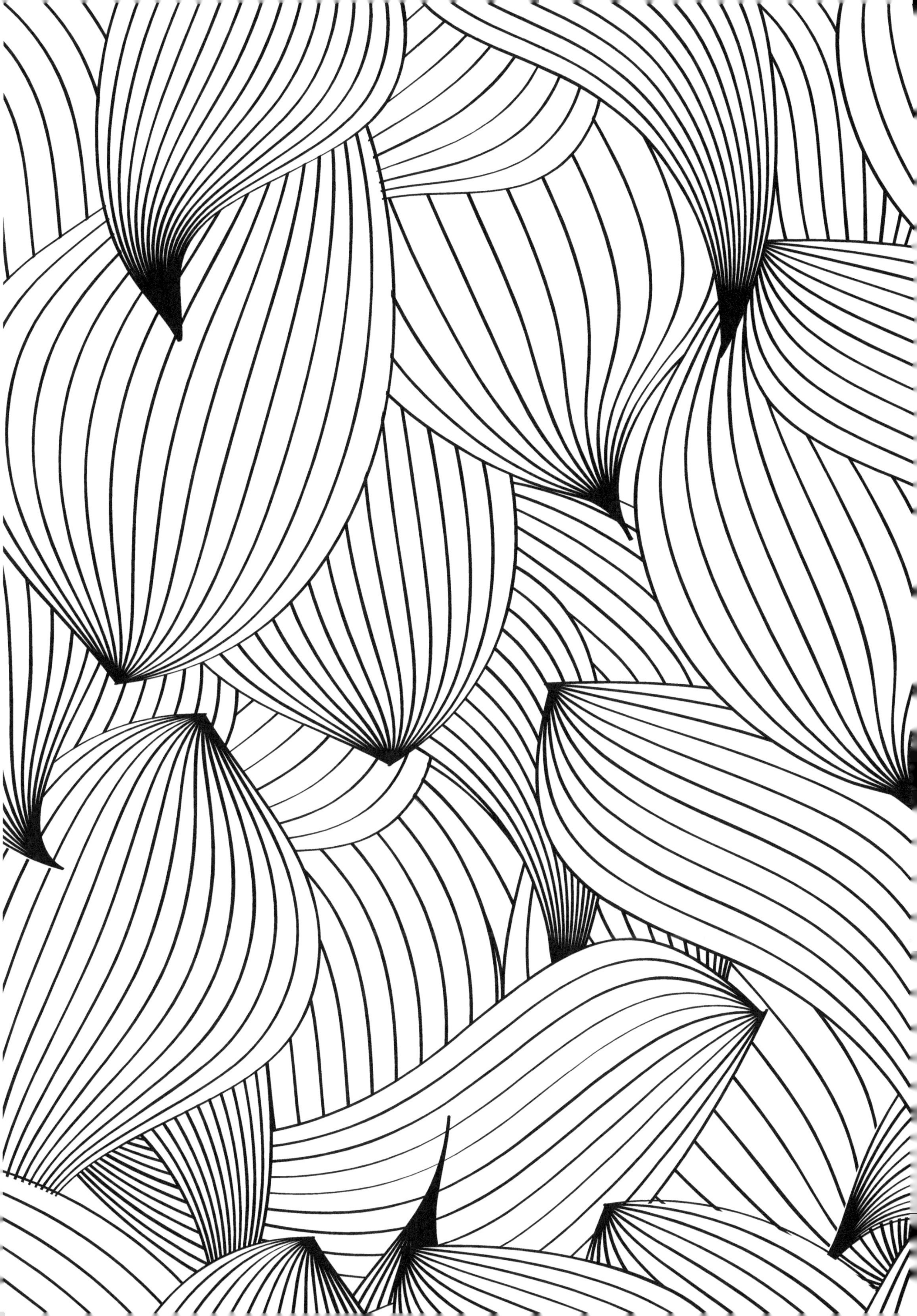

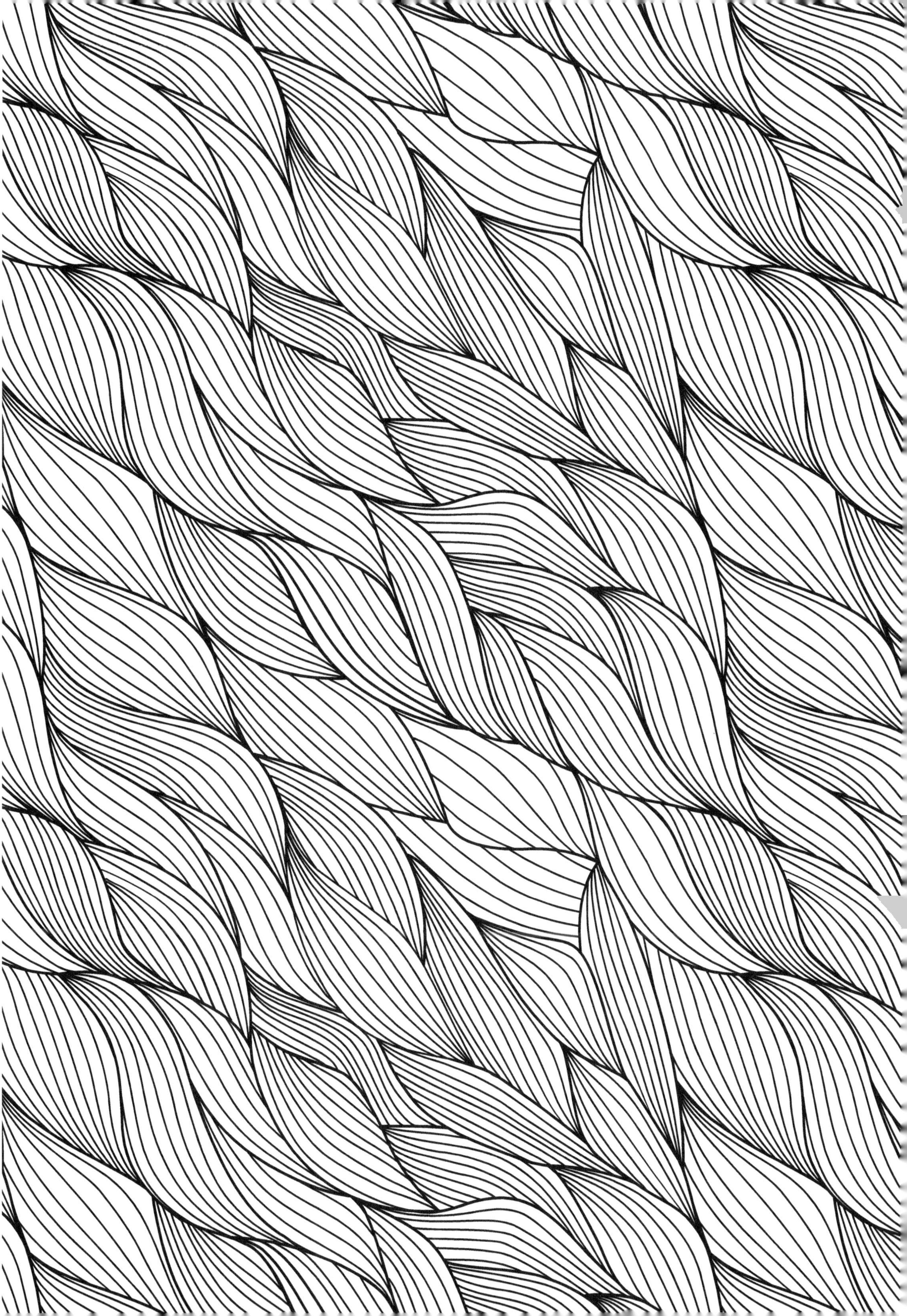

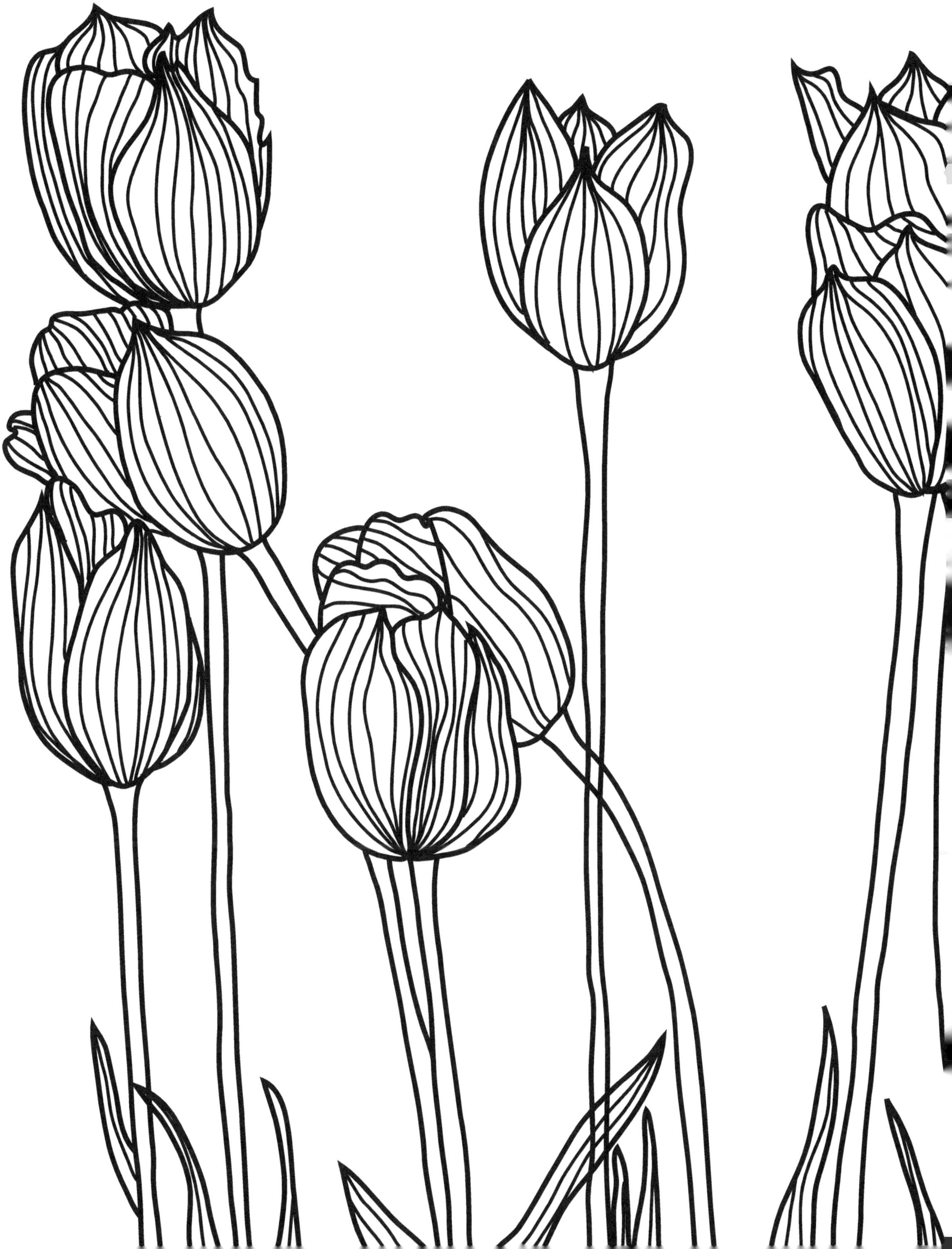

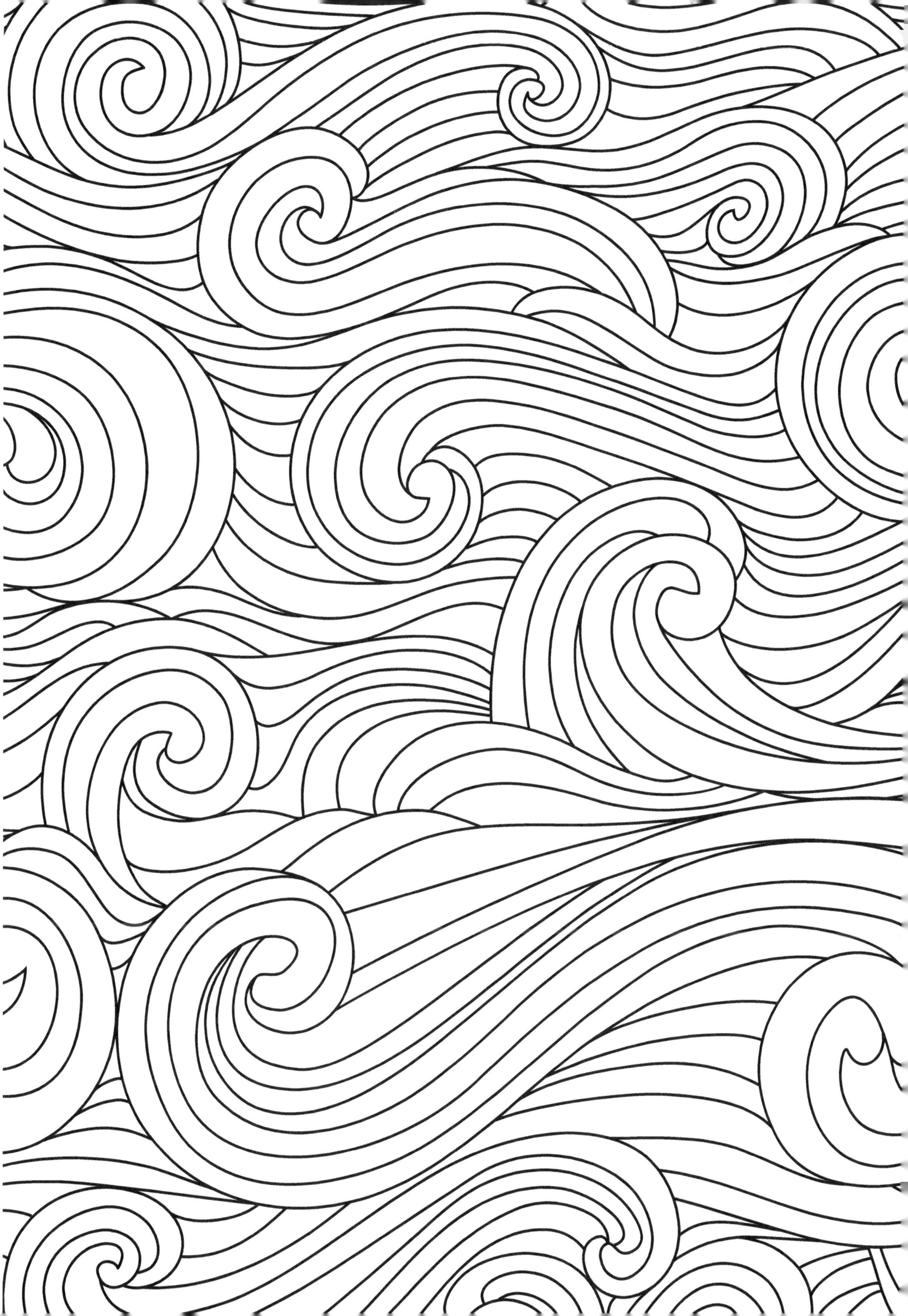

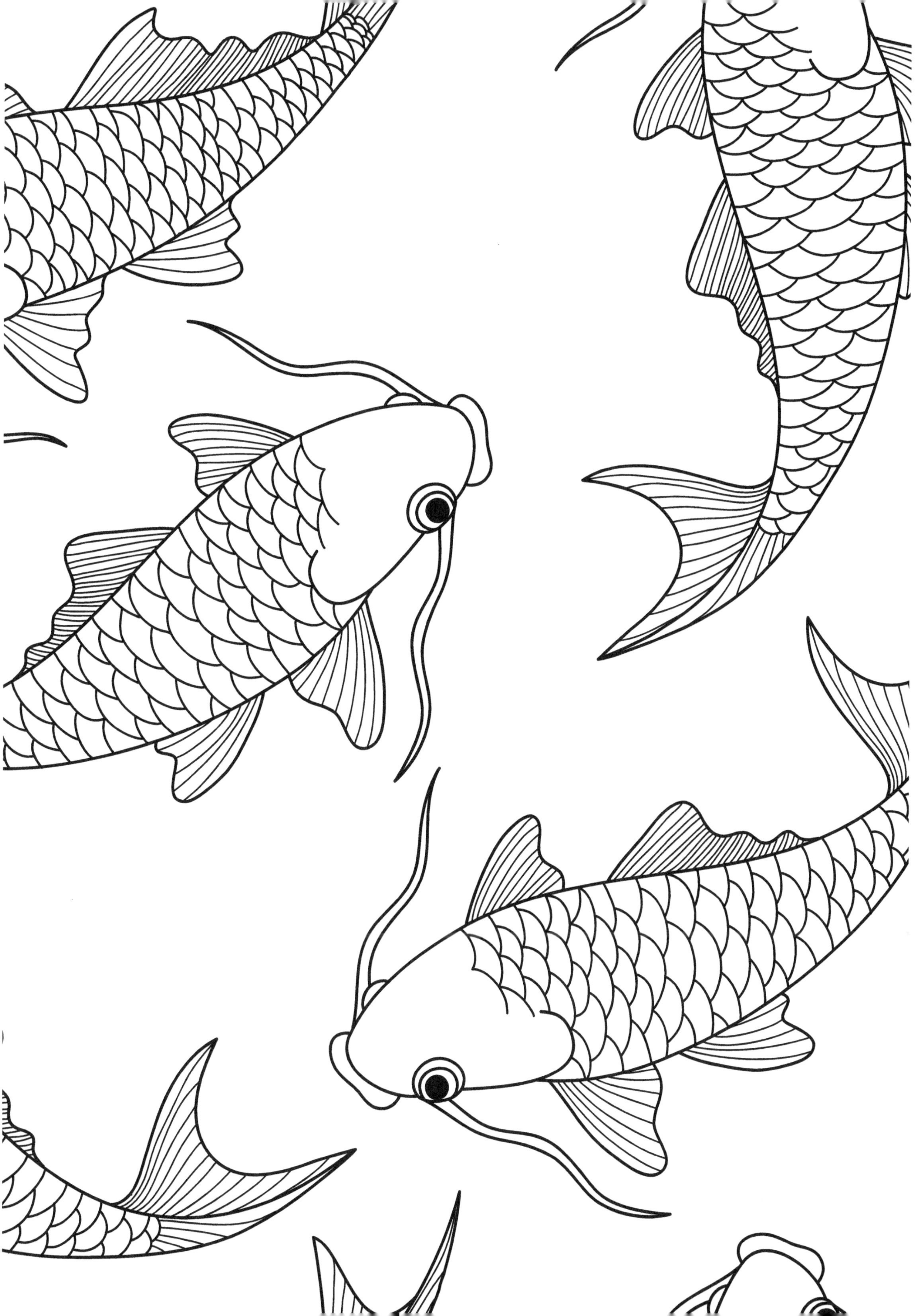

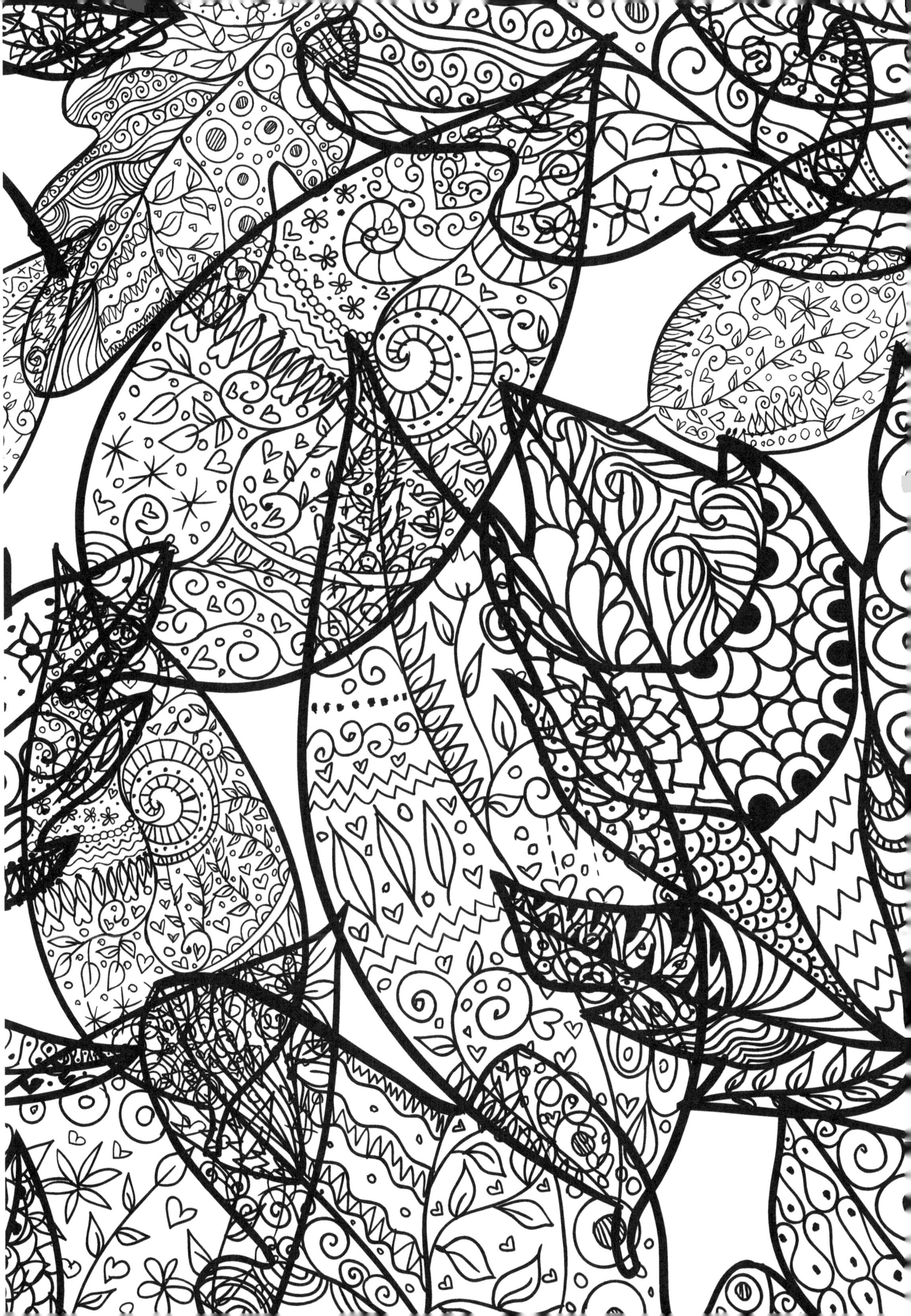

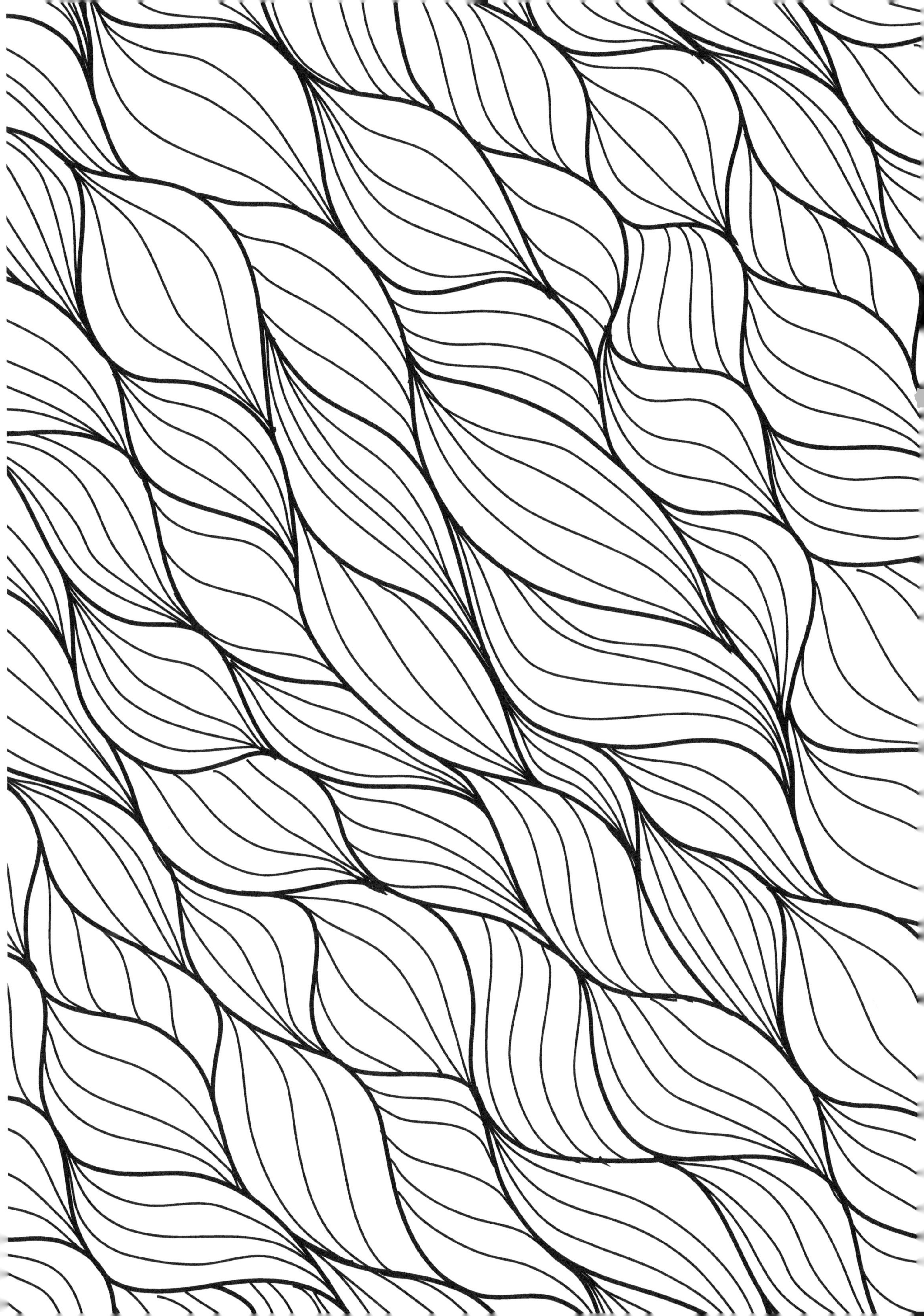

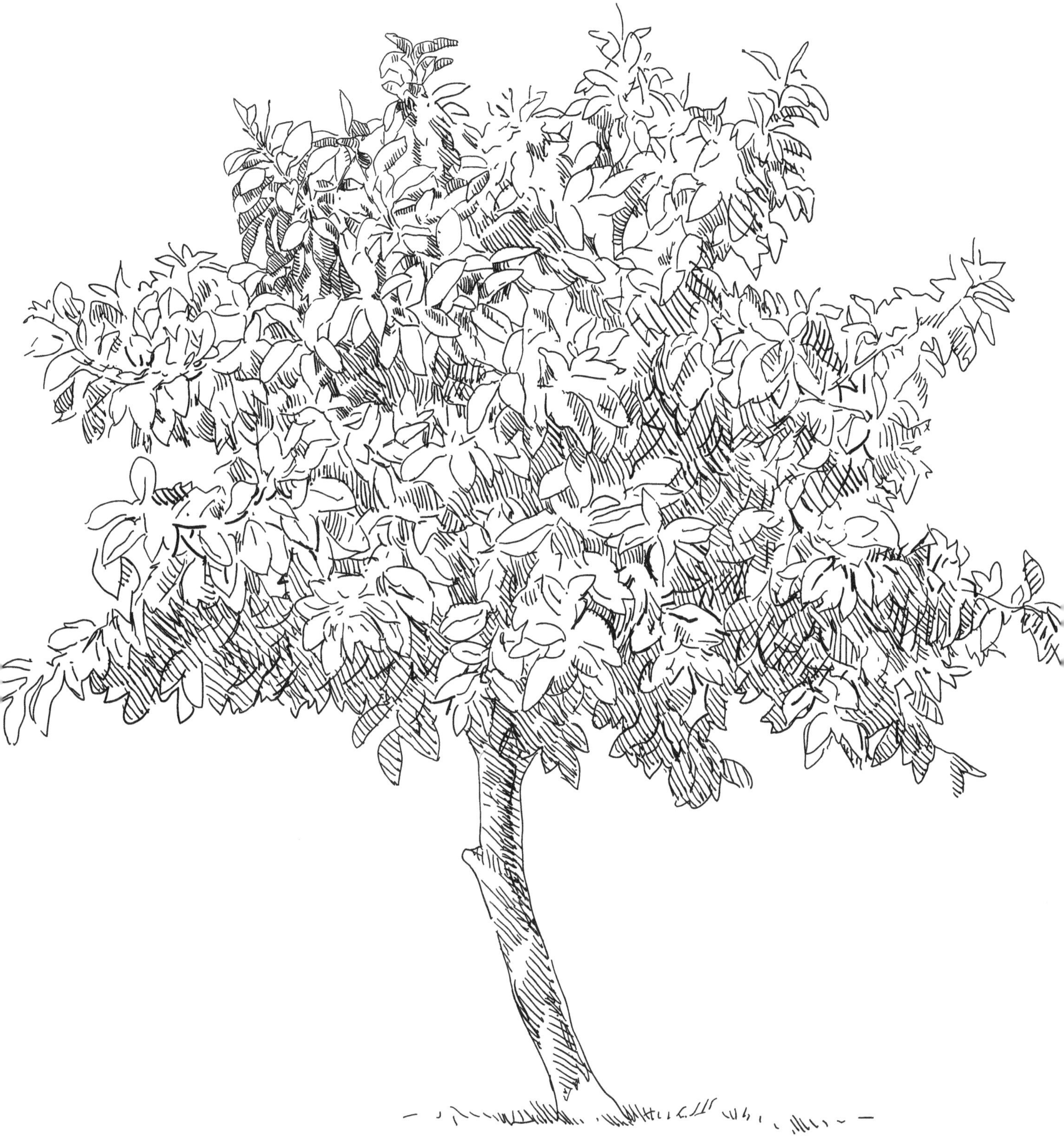

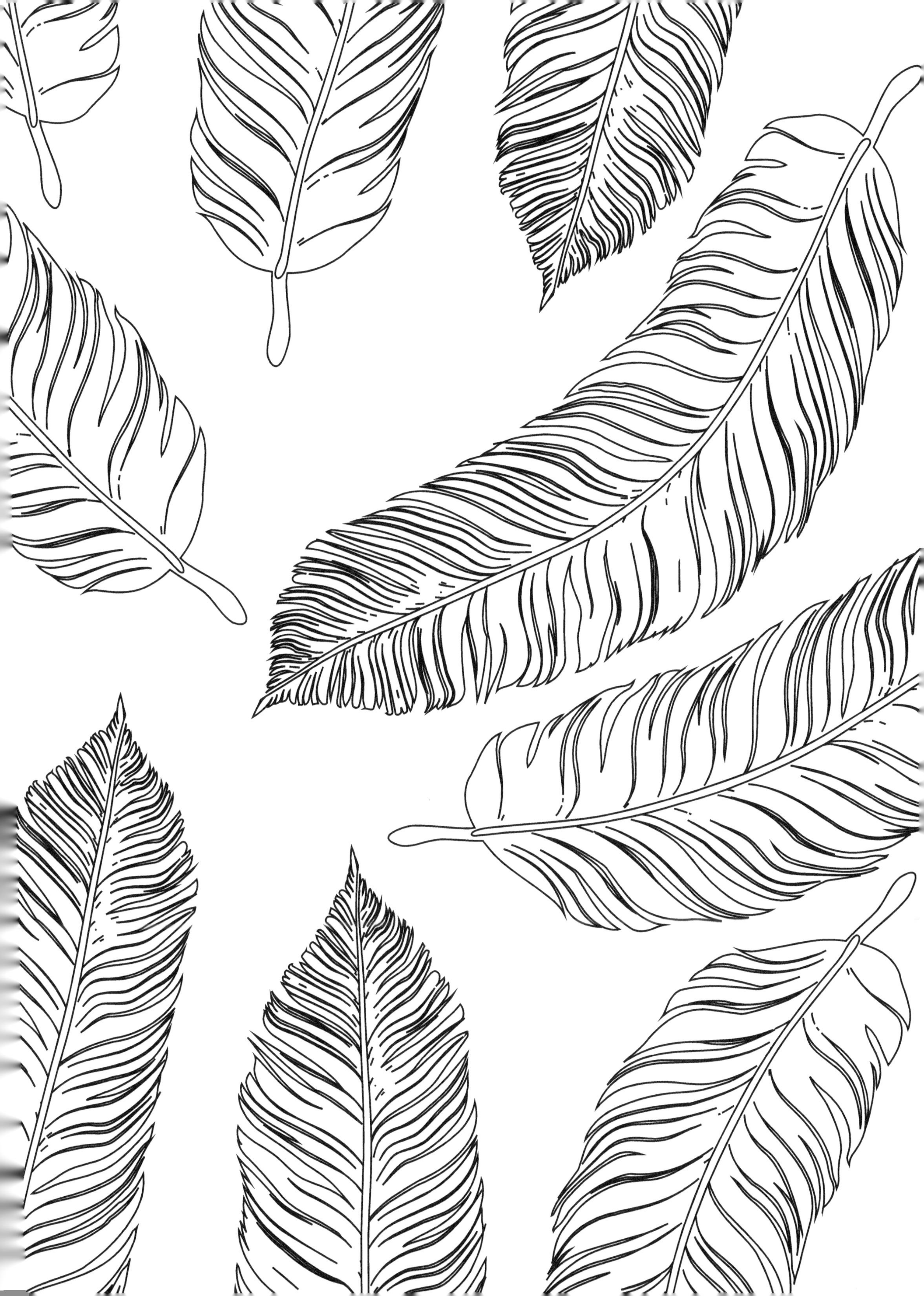

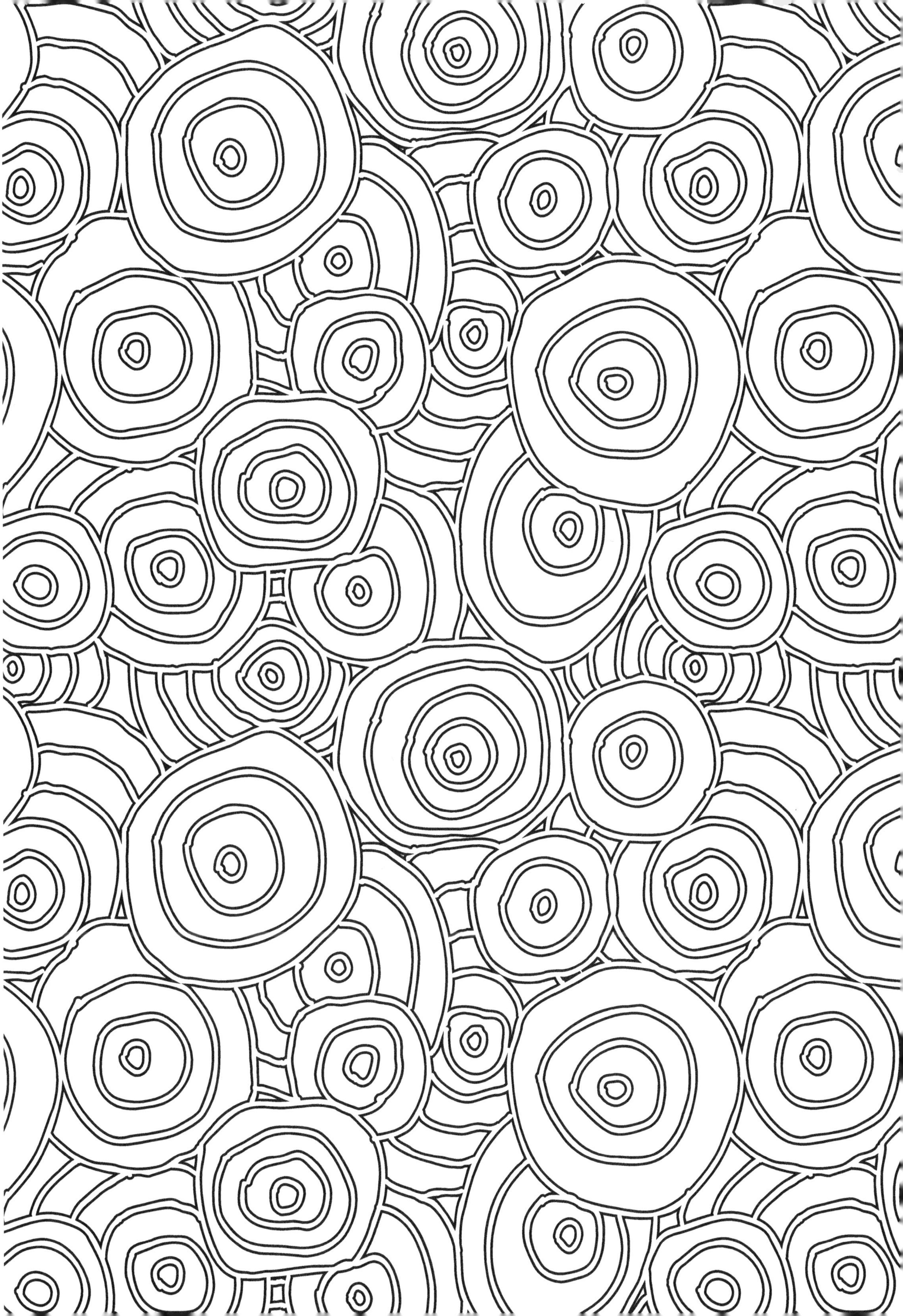

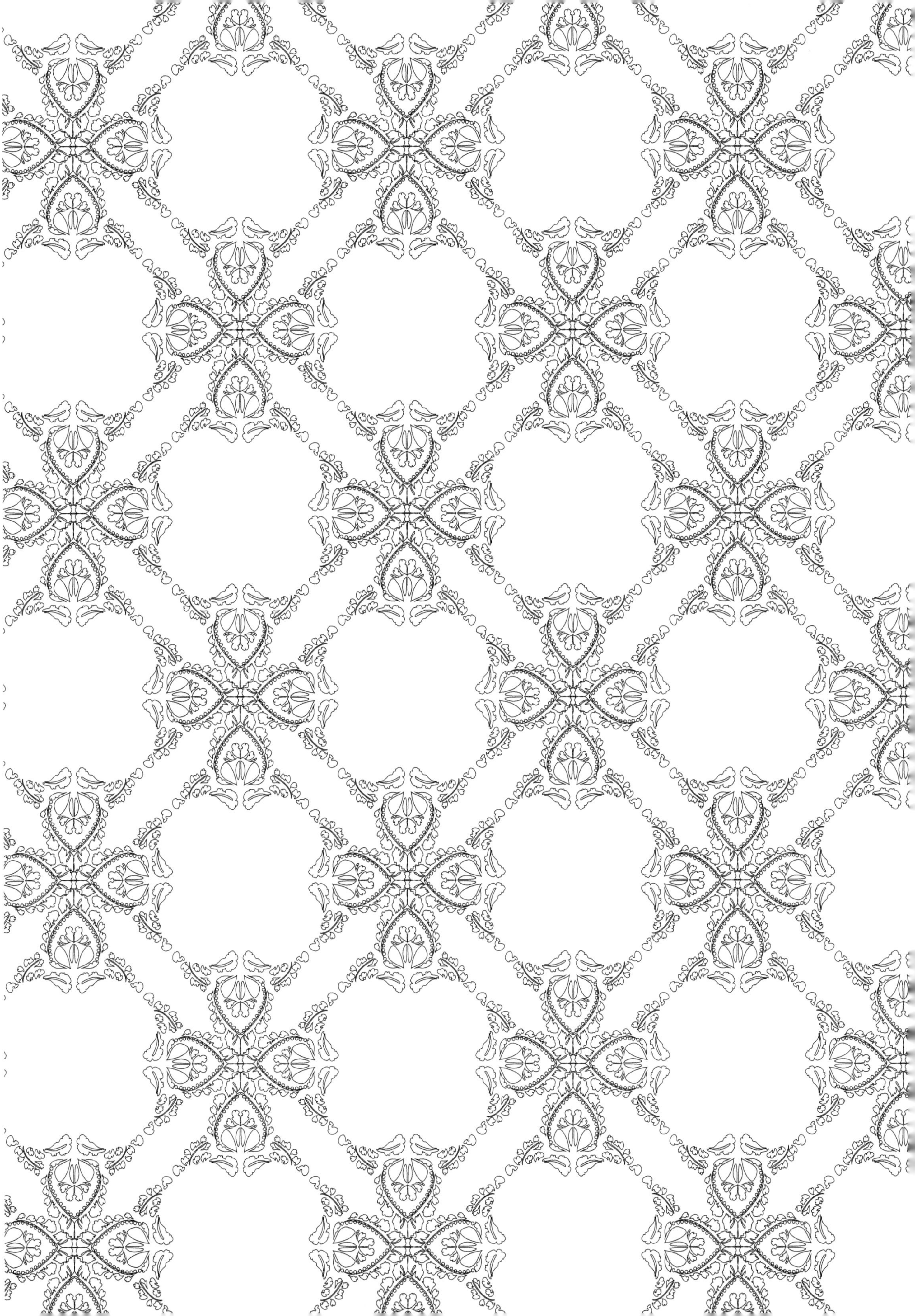

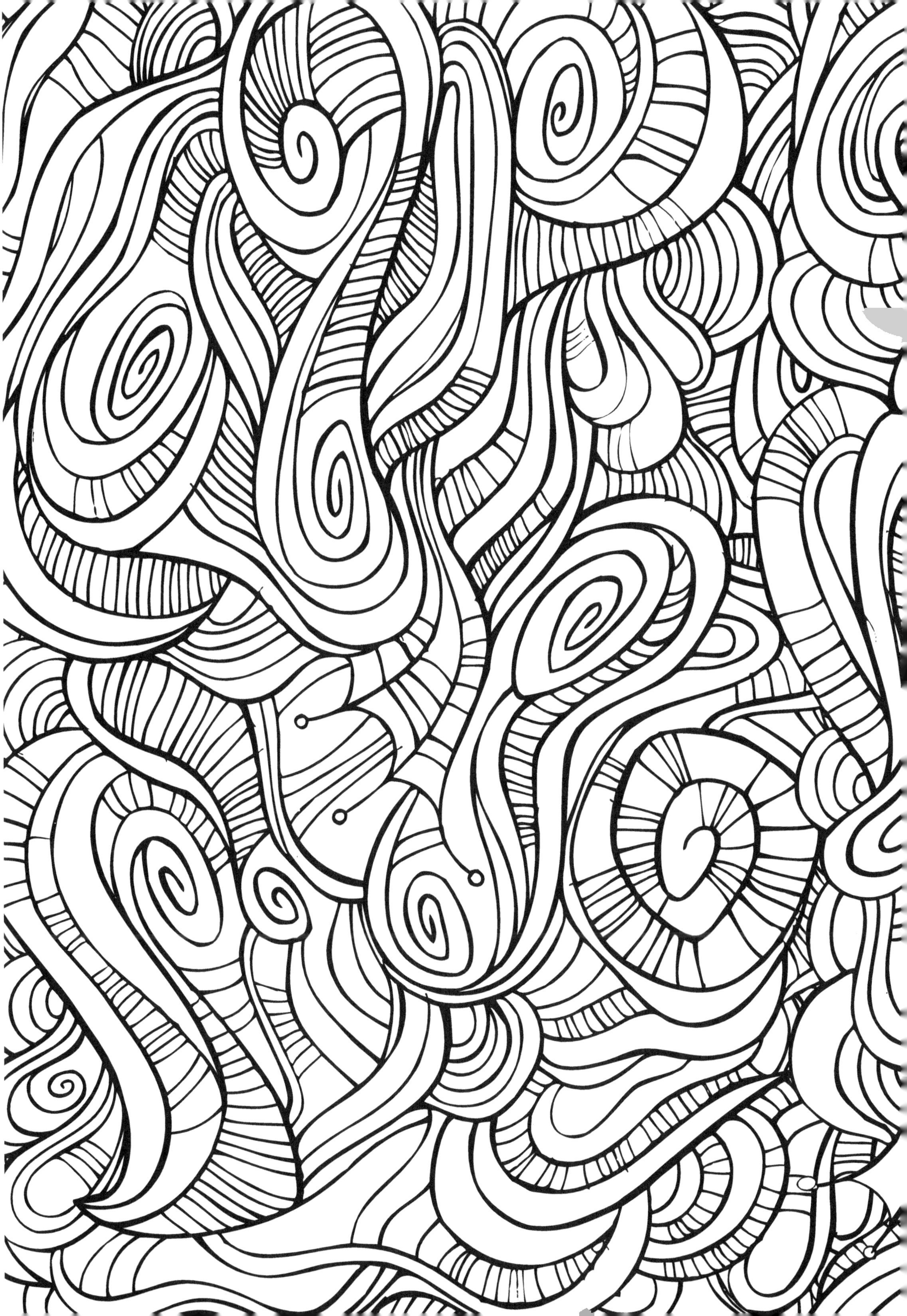

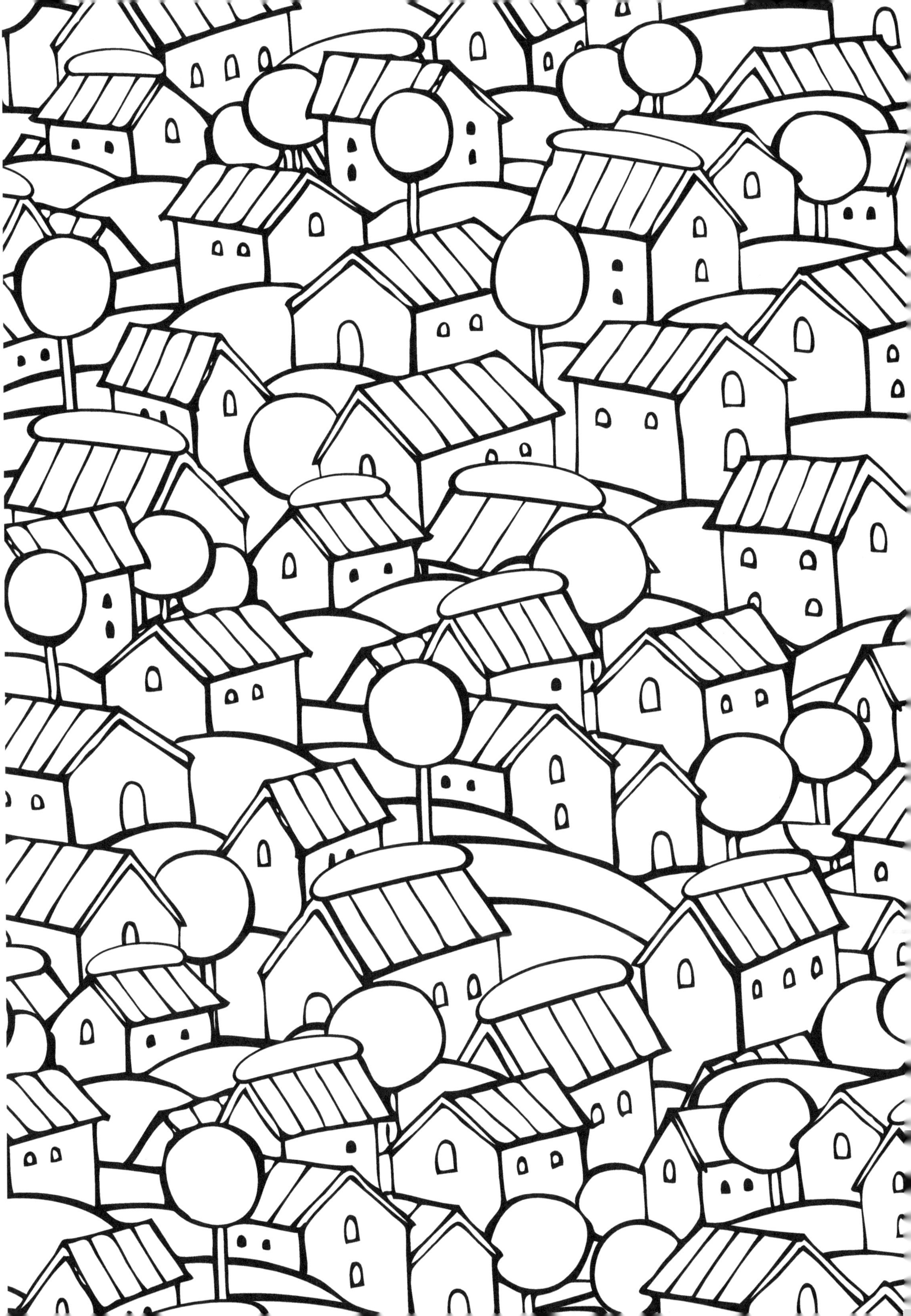

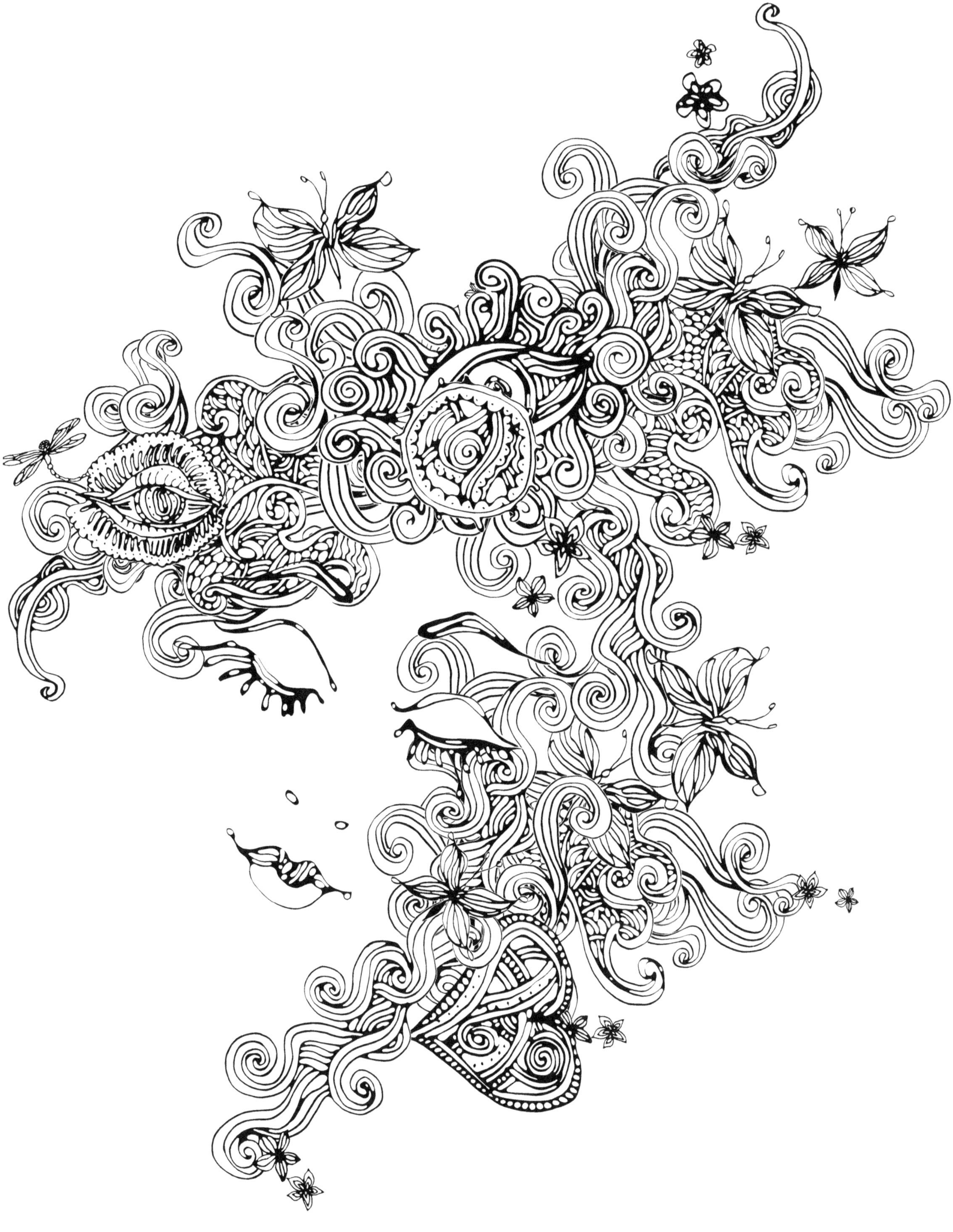

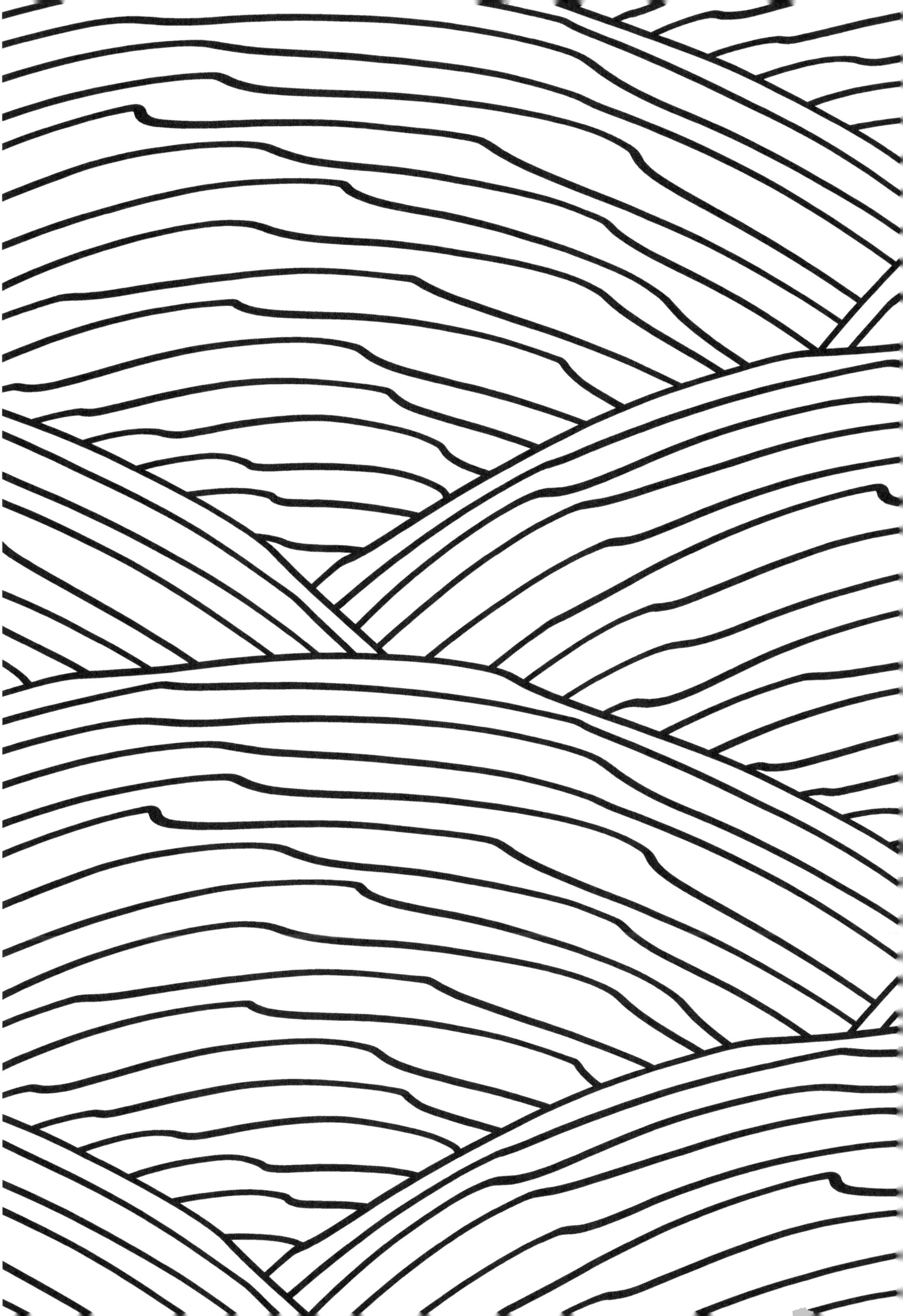

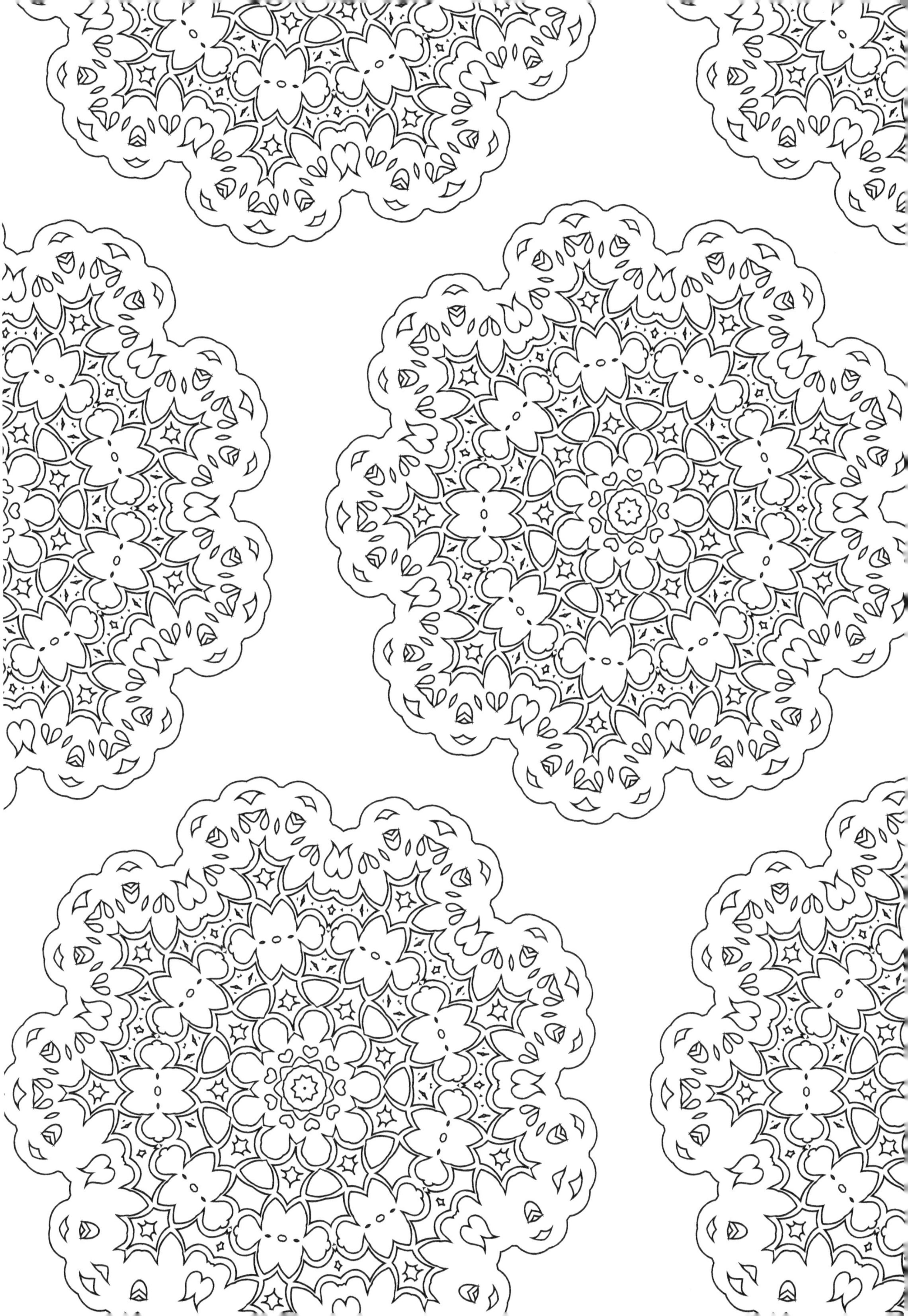

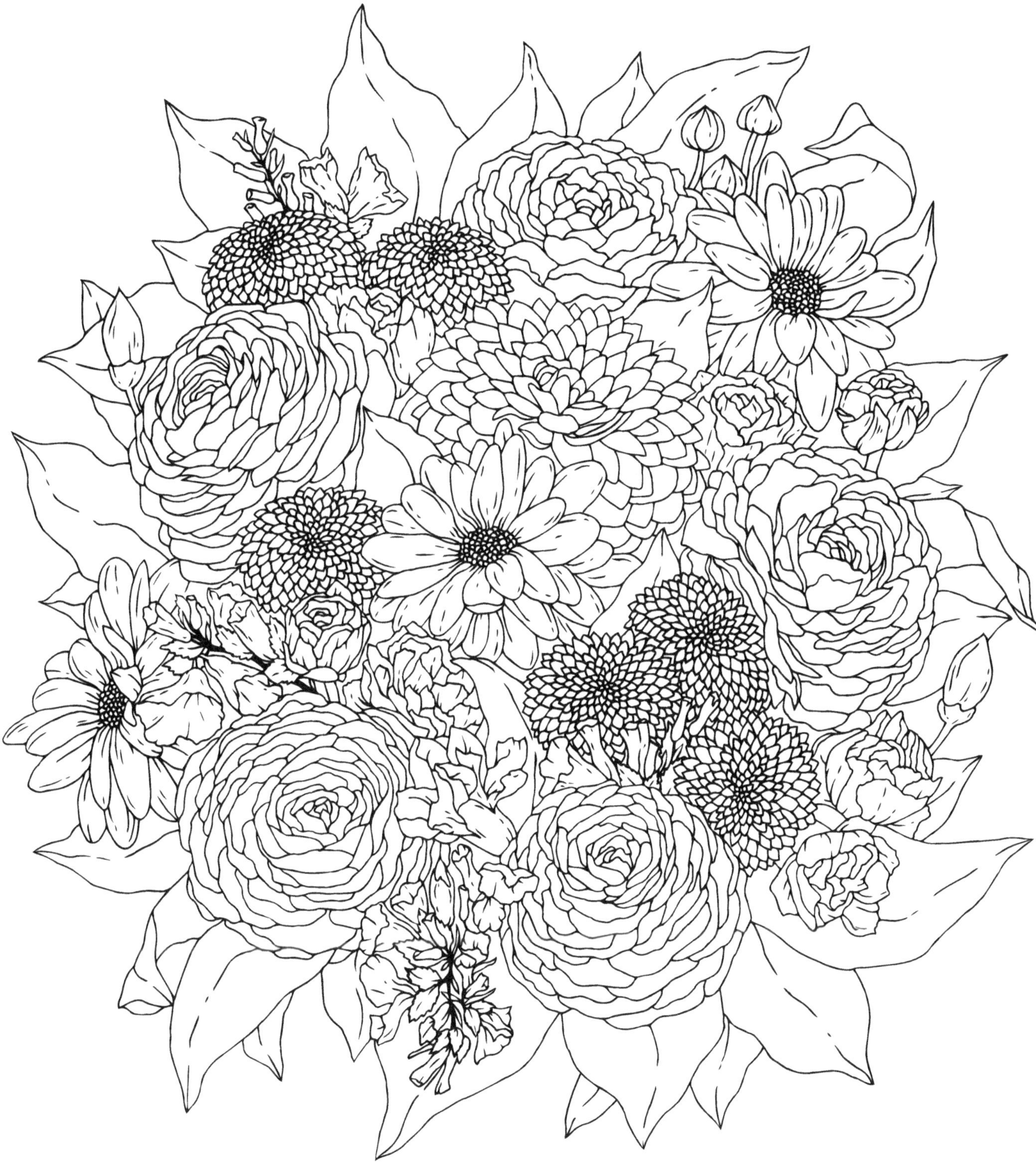

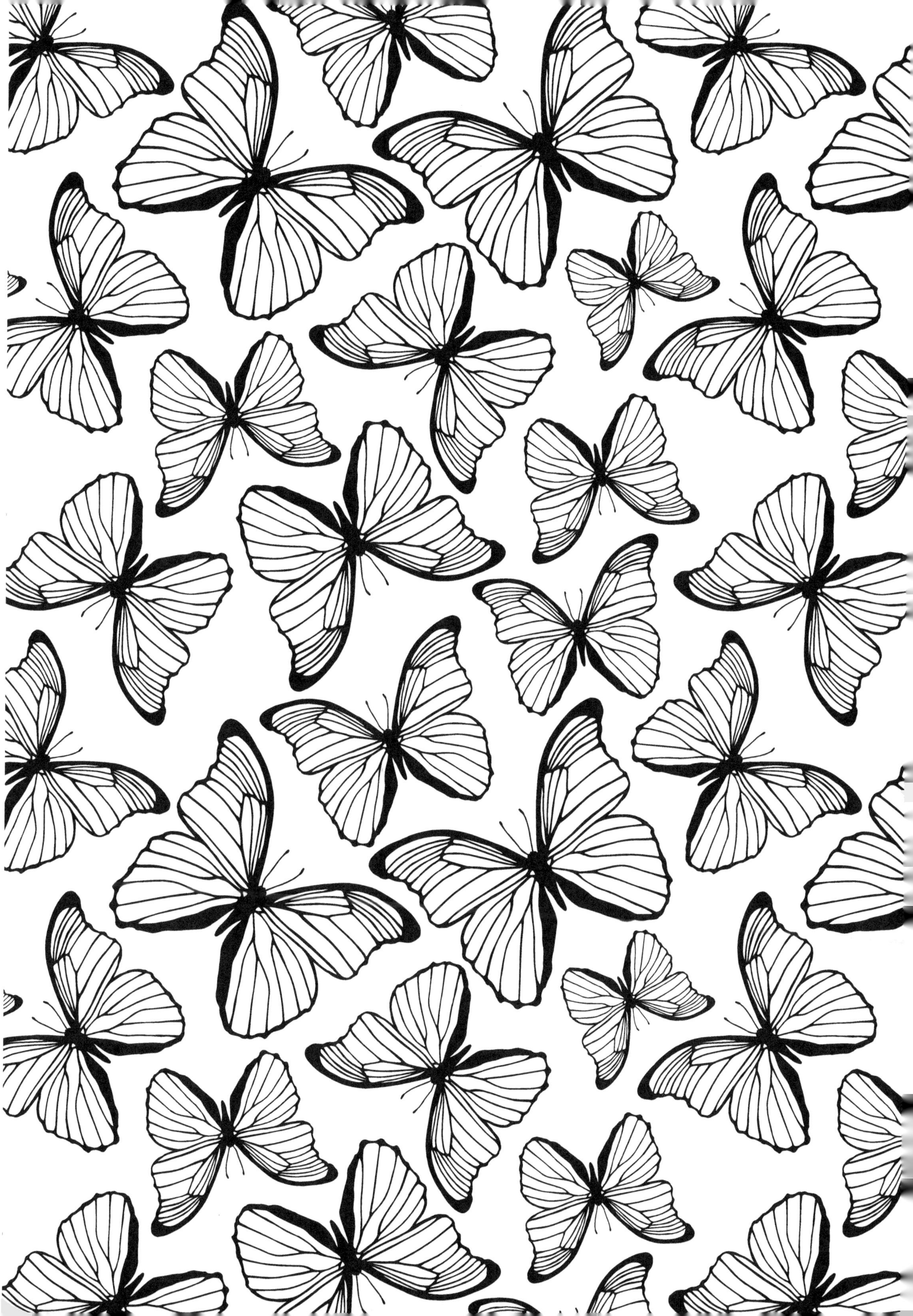

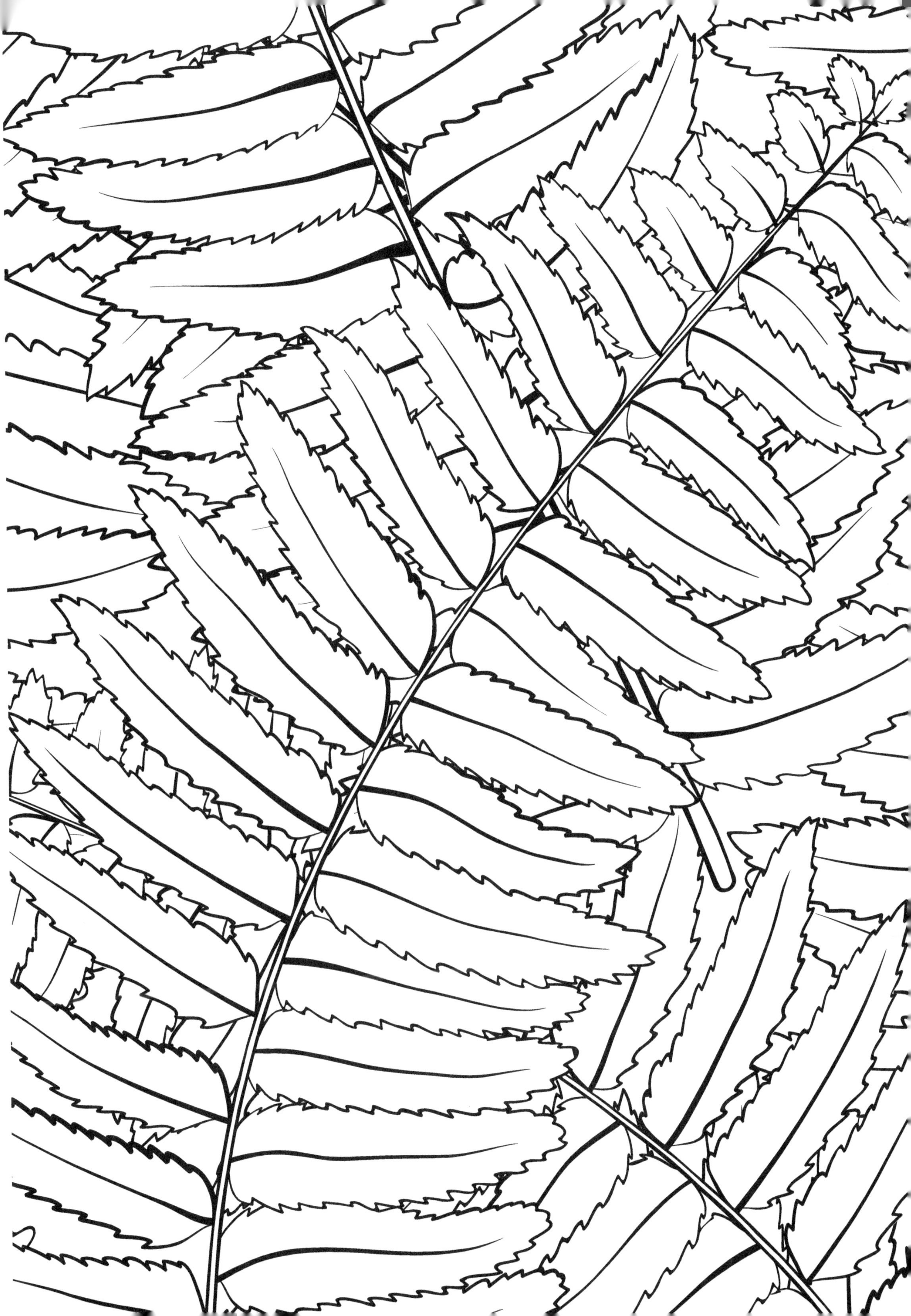

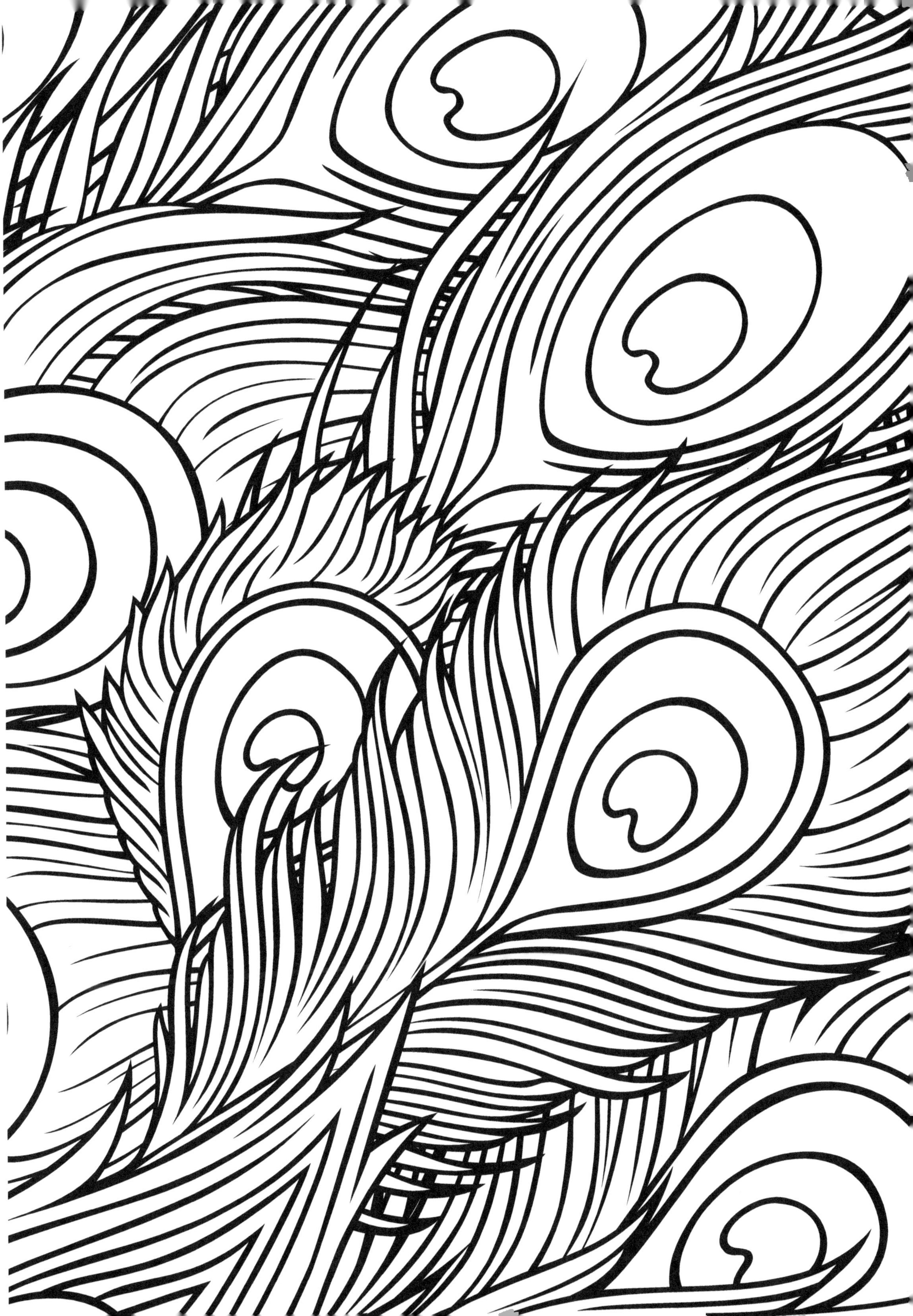

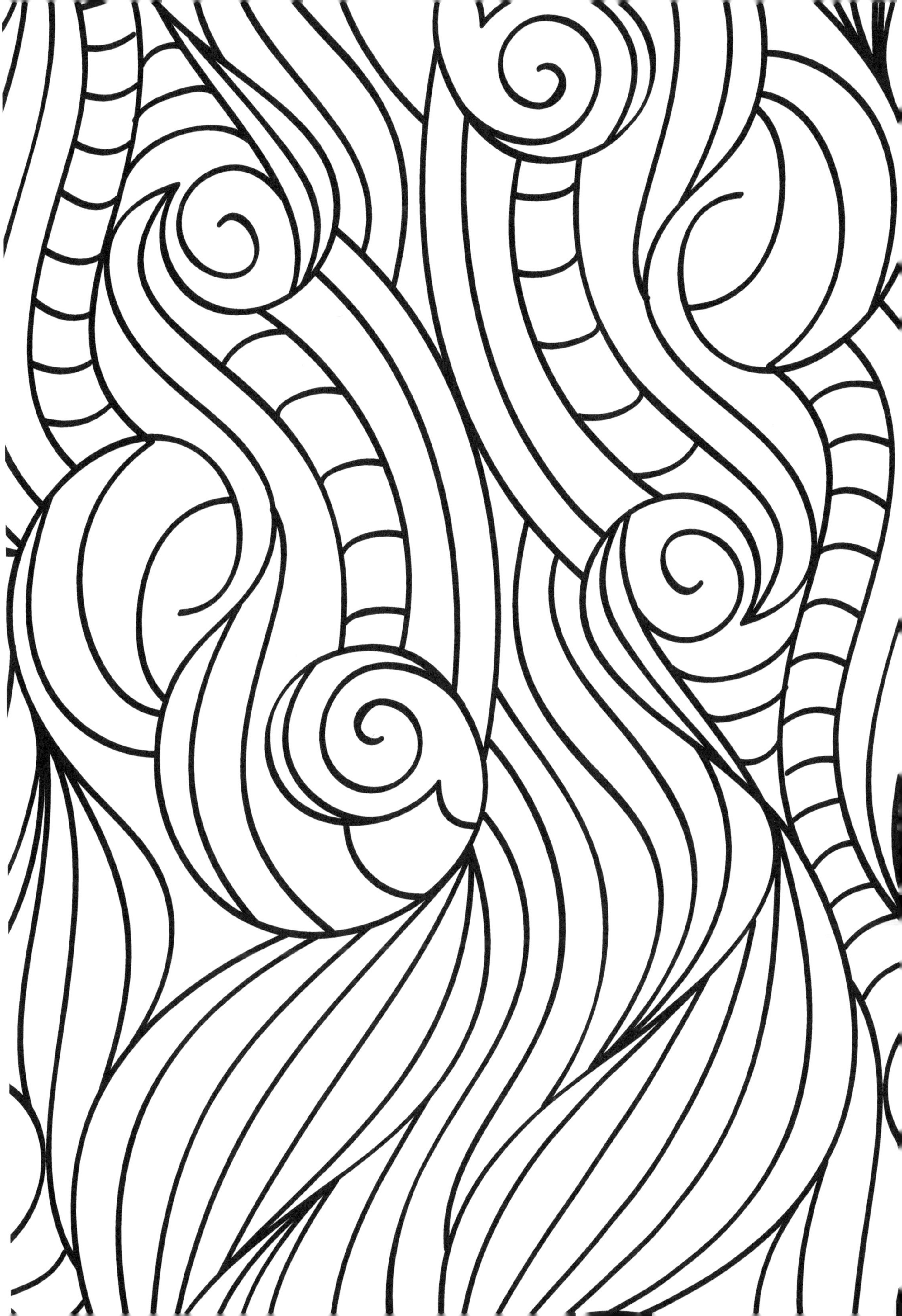

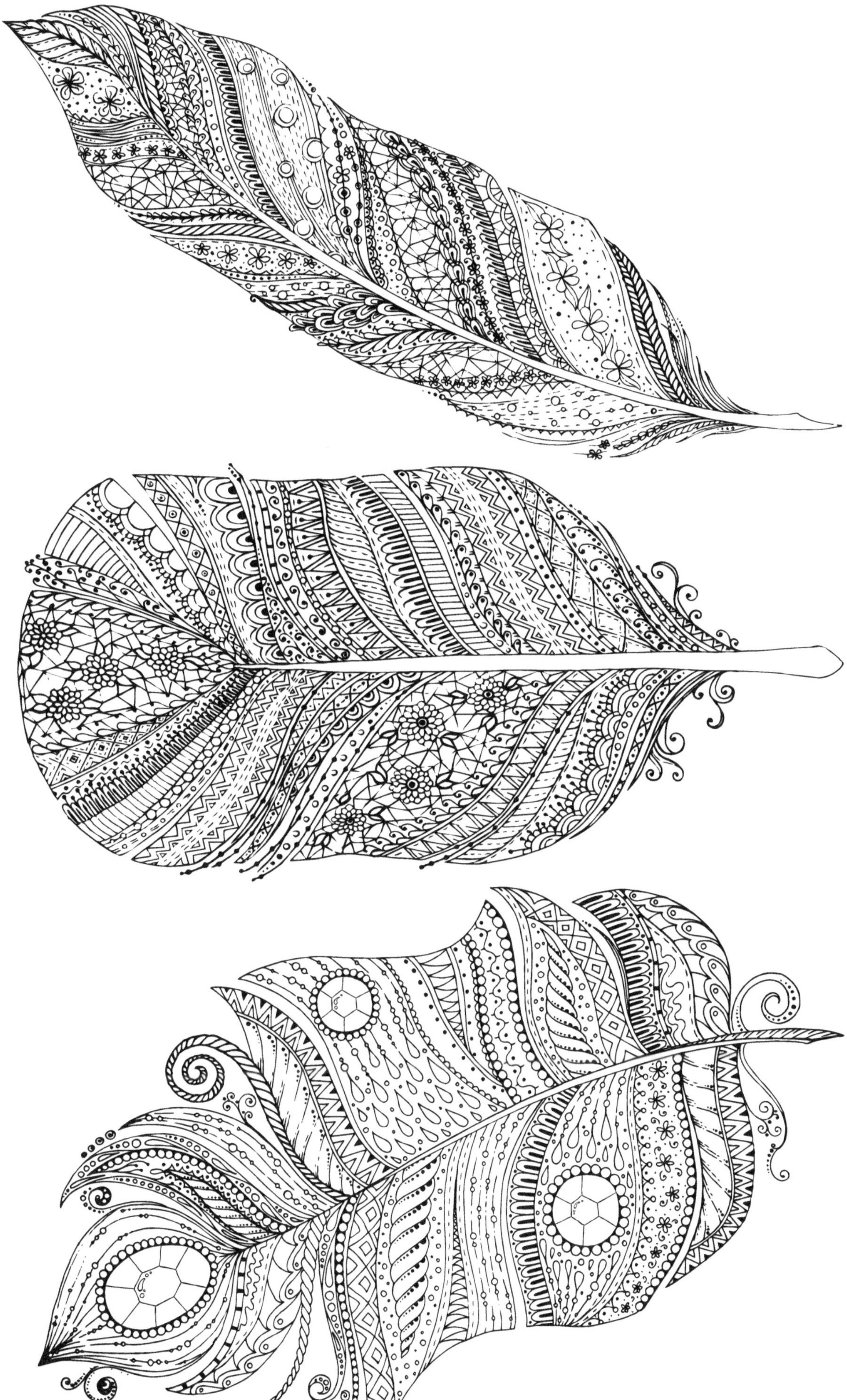

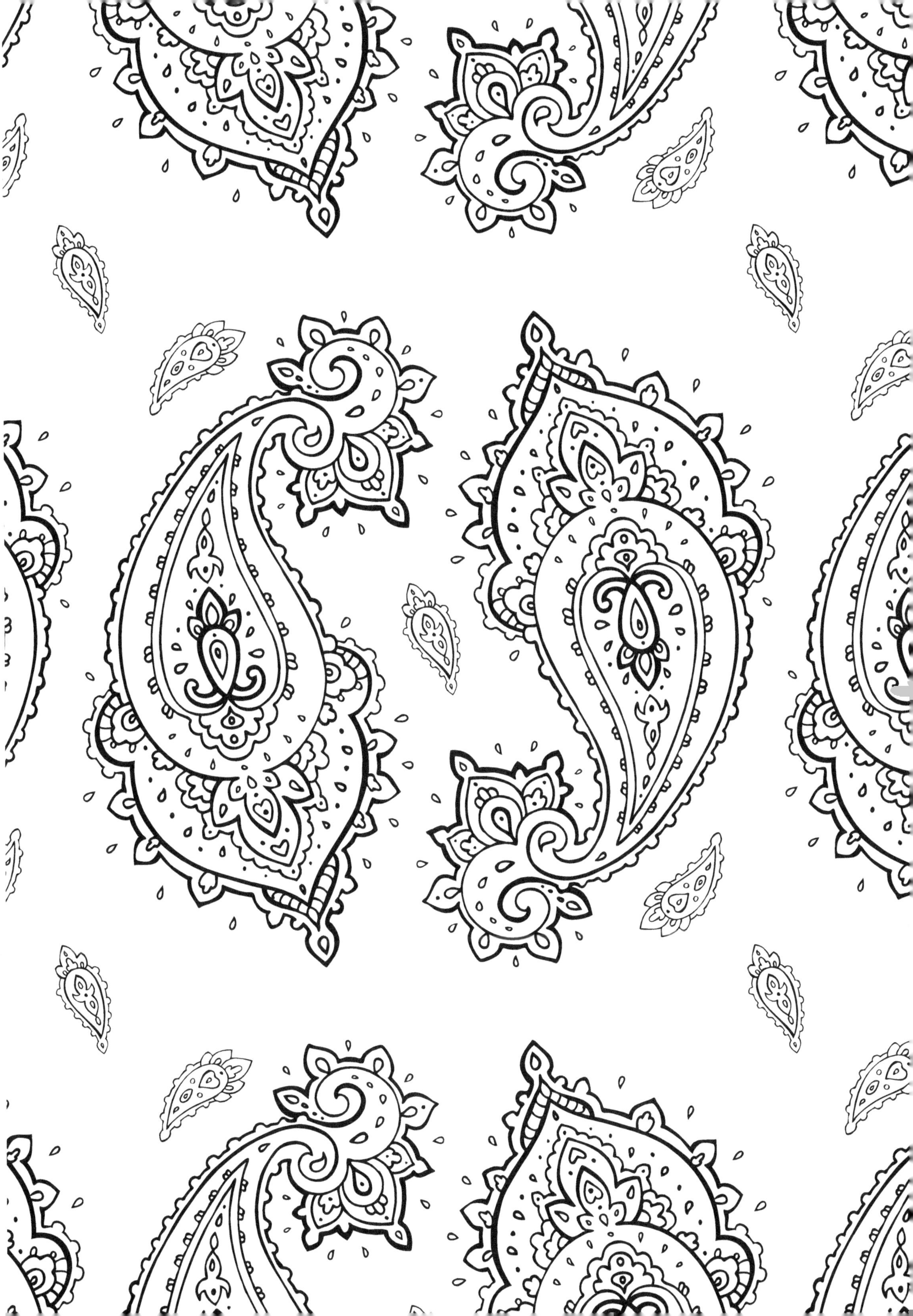

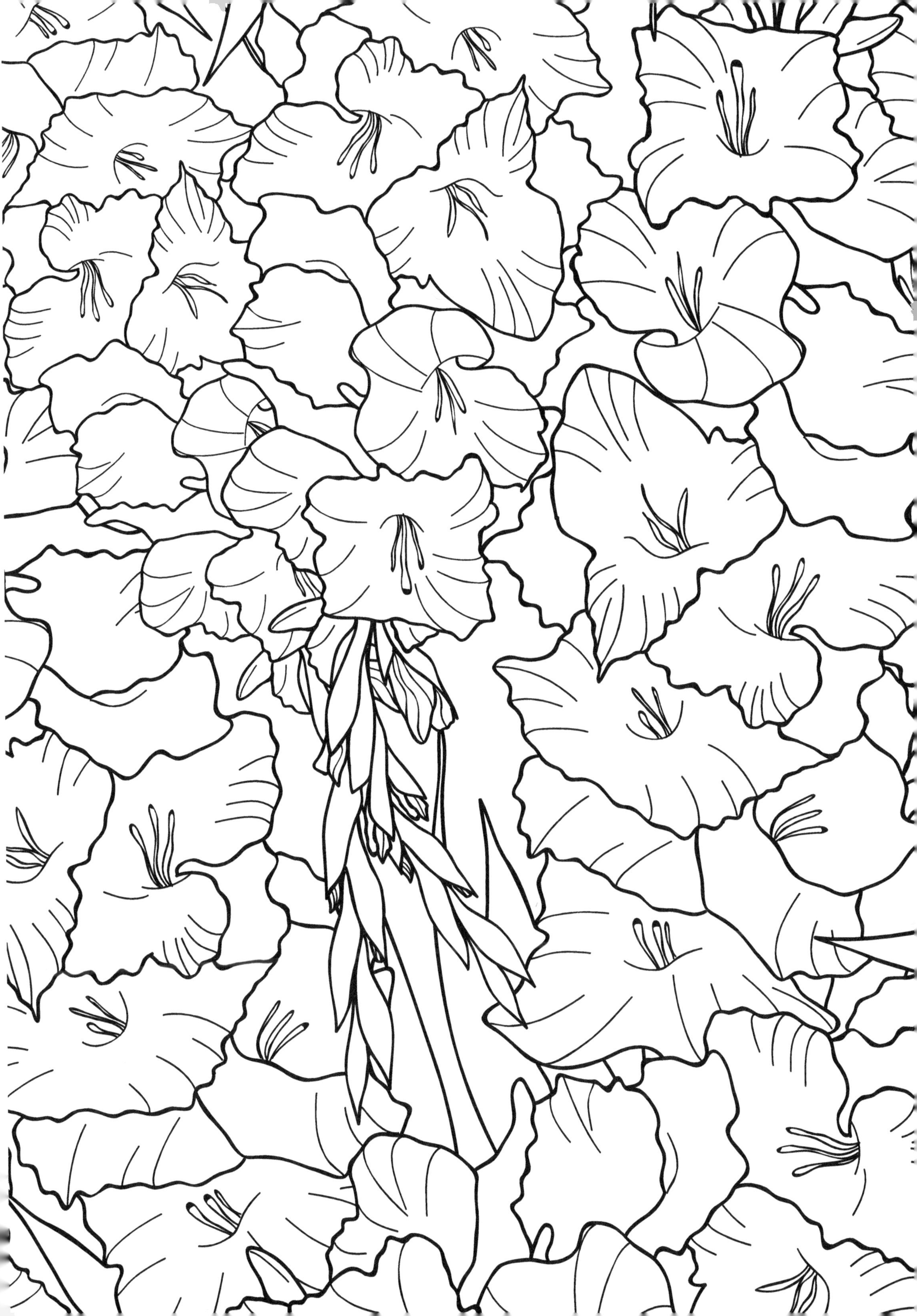

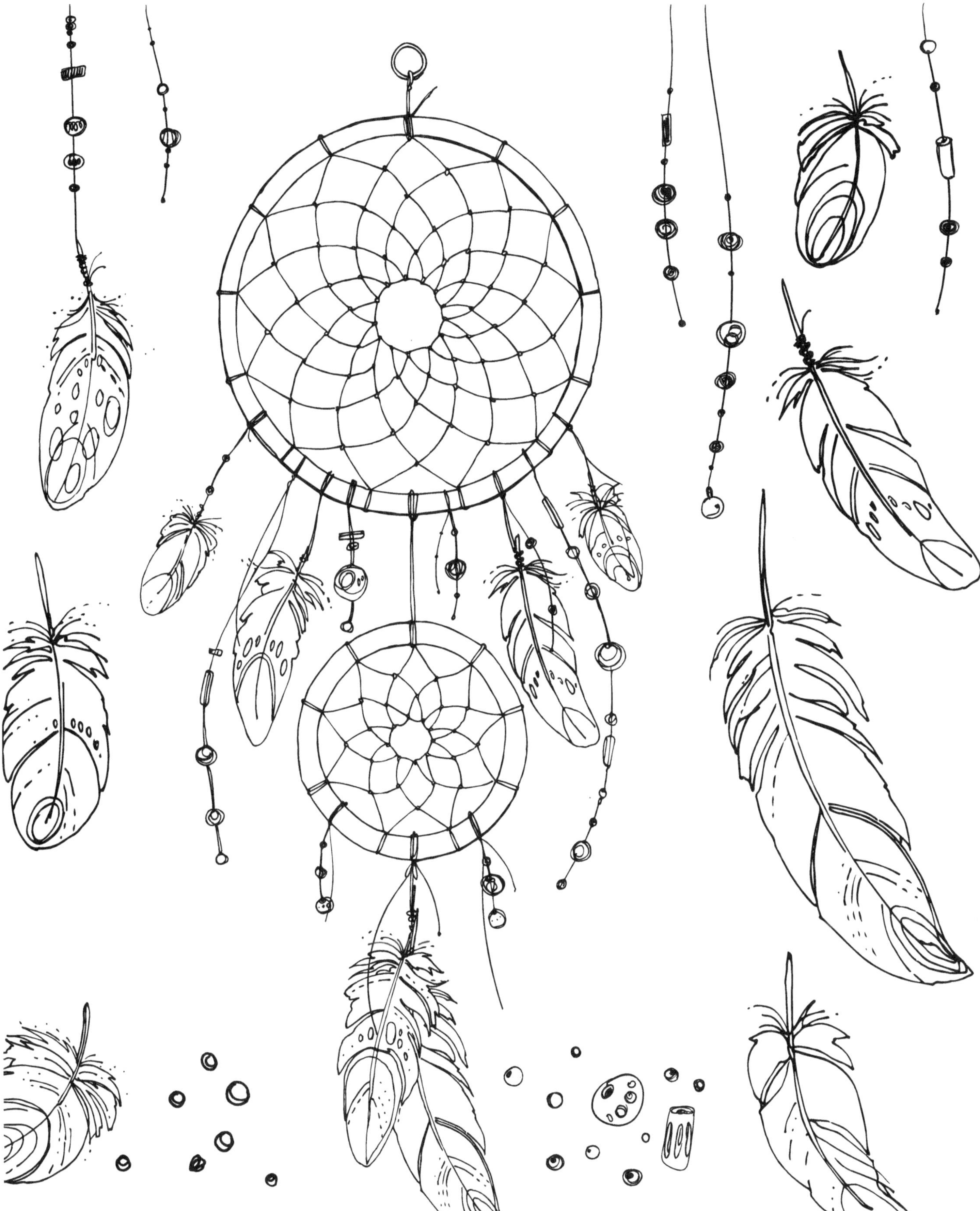

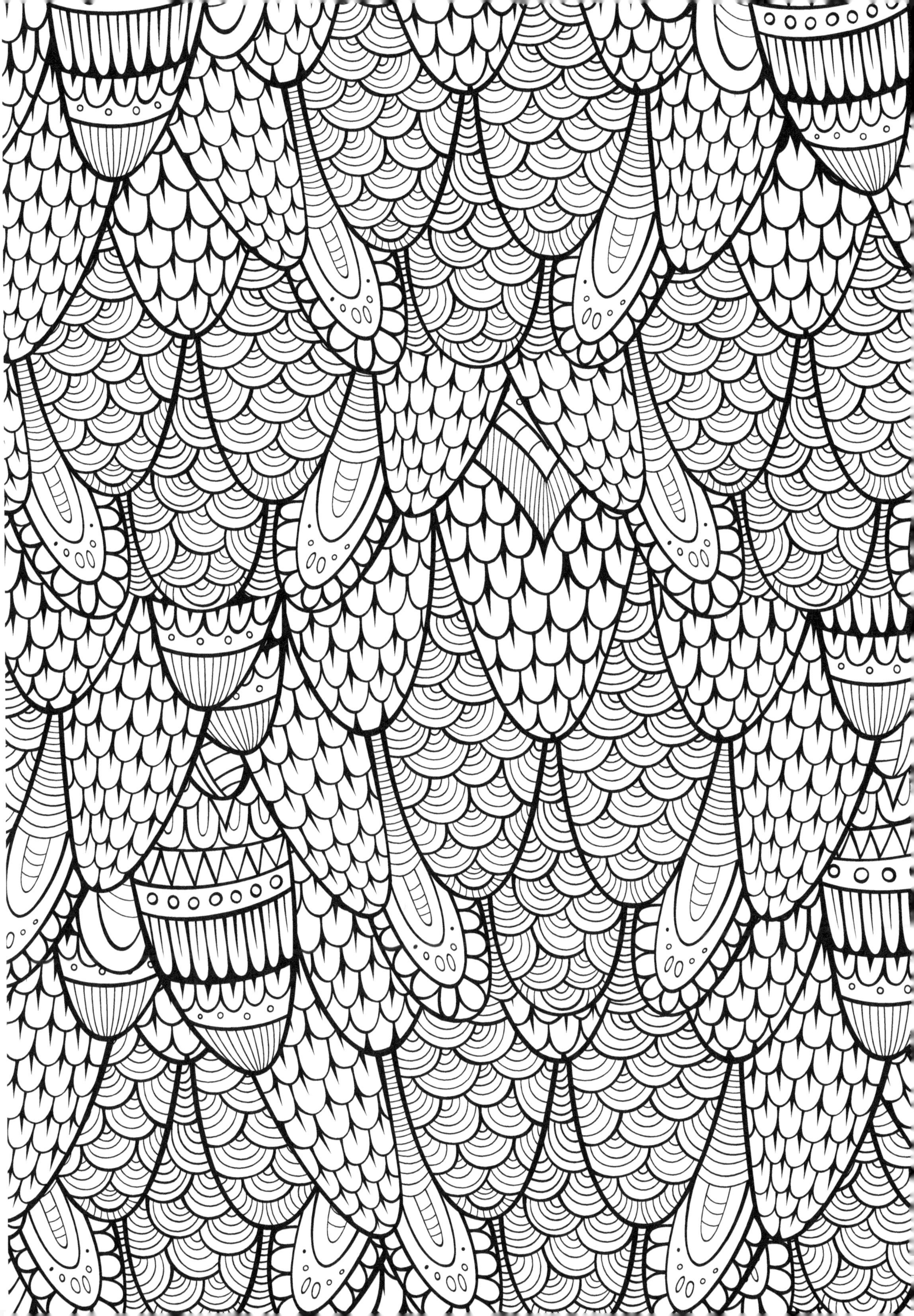

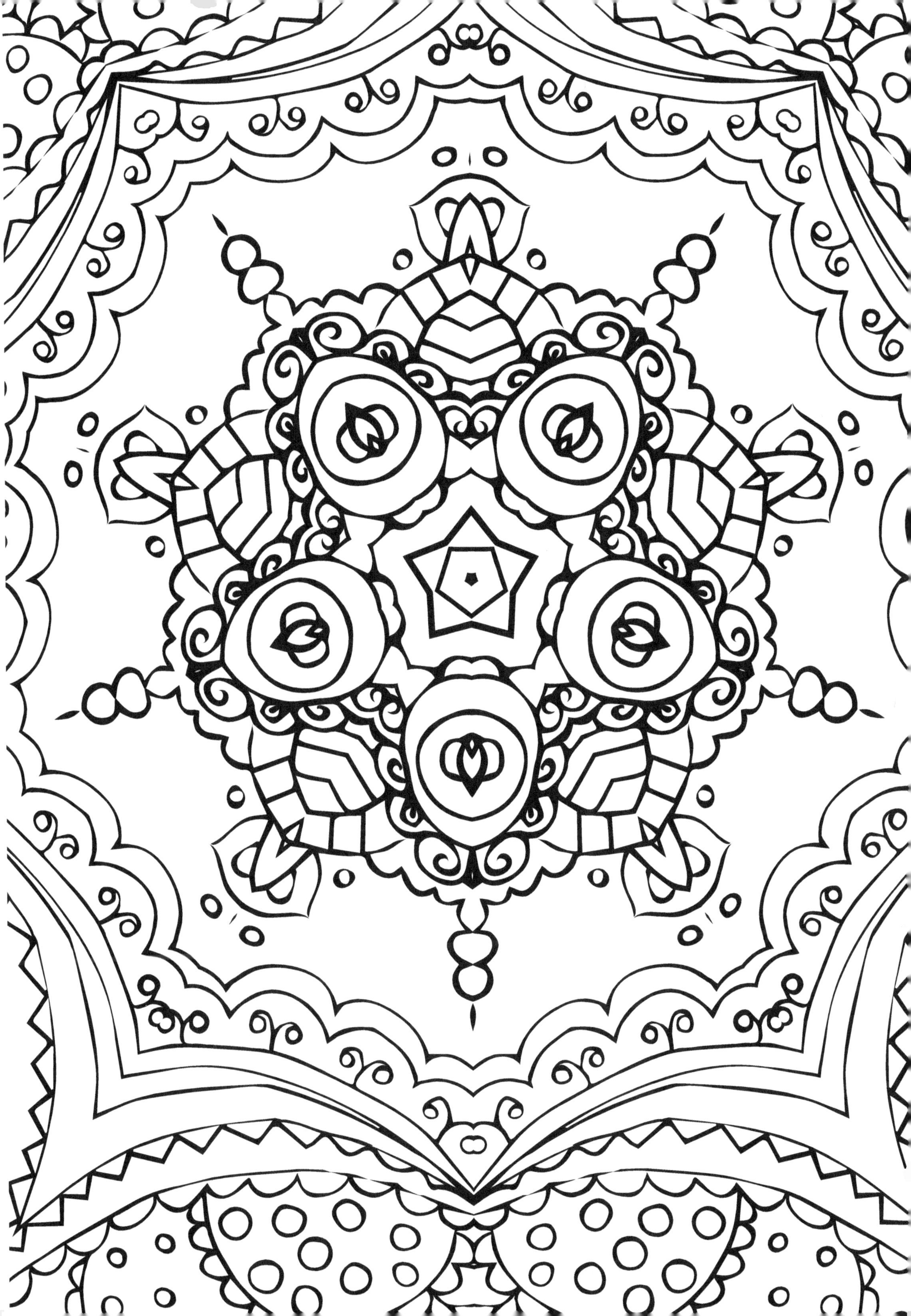

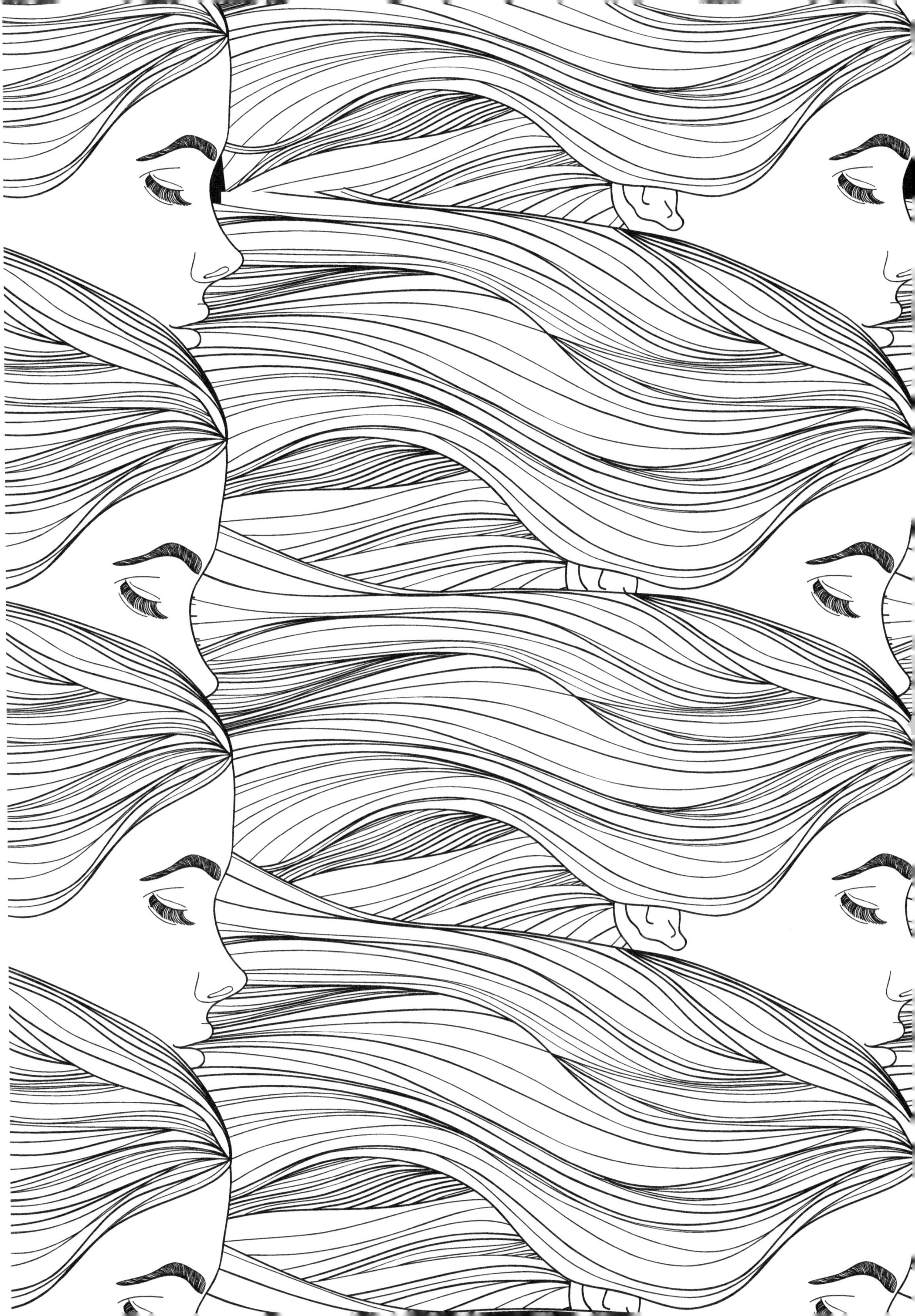

www.ingramcontent.com/pod-product-compliance
Lightning Source LLC
Chambersburg PA
CBHW062338220526
45469CB00008B/2758
* 9 7 8 1 7 8 5 9 5 0 7 2 8 *